Connected  Mathematics™

Covering and Surrounding

Two-Dimensional Measurement

Student Edition

D1278419

Glenda Lappan
James T. Fey
William M. Fitzgerald
Susan N. Friel
Elizabeth Difanis Phillips

PEARSON

Prentice Hall

Needham, Massachusetts
Upper Saddle River, New Jersey

The Connected Mathematics Project was developed at Michigan State University with the support of National Science Foundation Grant No. MDR 9150217.

This project was supported, in part,
by the
National Science Foundation
Opinions expressed are those of the authors
and not necessarily those of the Foundation

The Michigan State University authors and administration have agreed that all MSU royalties arising from this publication will be devoted to purposes supported by the Department of Mathematics and the MSU Mathematics Education Enrichment Fund.

Photo Acknowledgements: 6 © Hazel Hankin/Stock, Boston; 7© Hamilton Smith/FPG International; 19 © Michael Tamborrino/FPG International; 22 © Toyohiro Yamada/FPG International; 25© Ira Kirschenbaum/Stock, Boston; 29 © George Bellerose/Stock, Boston; 35 © Walter Sittig/The Image Works; 38 © Carrie Boretz/The Image Works; 59 © William B. Finch/Stock, Boston; 69 (umbrellas) © Owen Franken/Stock, Boston; 69 (manhole) © Peter Vandermark/Stock, Boston; 69 (dog) © Peter Southwick/Stock, Boston; 70 © Barbara Alper/Stock, Boston; 75 © Mark Antman/The Image Works

PEARSON
Prentice
Hall

ISBN 0-13-180809-5
5 6 7 8 9 10   07 06 05

The Connected Mathematics Project Staff

Project Directors

James T. Fey
University of Maryland

William M. Fitzgerald
Michigan State University

Susan N. Friel
University of North Carolina at Chapel Hill

Glenda Lappan
Michigan State University

Elizabeth Difanis Phillips
Michigan State University

Project Manager

Kathy Burgis
Michigan State University

Technical Coordinator

Judith Martus Miller
Michigan State University

Curriculum Development Consultants

David Ben-Chaim
Weizmann Institute

Alex Friedlander
Weizmann Institute

Eleanor Geiger
University of Maryland

Jane Mitchell
University of North Carolina at Chapel Hill

Anthony D. Rickard
Alma College

Collaborating Teachers/Writers

Mary K. Bouck
Portland, Michigan

Jacqueline Stewart
Okemos, Michigan

Graduate Assistants

Scott J. Baldridge
Michigan State University

Angie S. Eshelman
Michigan State University

M. Faaiz Gierdien
Michigan State University

Jane M. Keiser
Indiana University

Angela S. Krebs
Michigan State University

James M. Larson
Michigan State University

Ronald Preston
Indiana University

Tat Ming Sze
Michigan State University

Sarah Theule-Lubienski
Michigan State University

Jeffrey J. Wanko
Michigan State University

Evaluation Team

Mark Hoover
Michigan State University

Diane V. Lambdin
Indiana University

Sandra K. Wilcox
Michigan State University

Judith S. Zawojewski
National-Louis University

Teacher/Assessment Team

Kathy Booth
Waverly, Michigan

Anita Clark
Marshall, Michigan

Theodore Gardella
Bloomfield Hills, Michigan

Yvonne Grant
Portland, Michigan

Linda R. Lobue
Vista, California

Suzanne McGrath
Chula Vista, California

Nancy McIntyre
Troy, Michigan

Linda Walker
Tallahassee, Florida

Software Developer

Richard Burgis
East Lansing, Michigan

Development Center Directors

Nicholas Branca
San Diego State University

Dianne Briars
Pittsburgh Public Schools

Frances R. Curcio
New York University

Perry Lanier
Michigan State University

J. Michael Shaughnessy
Portland State University

Charles Vonder Embse
Central Michigan University

Special thanks to the students and teachers at these pilot schools!

Baker Demonstration School
Evanston, Illinois

Bertha Vos Elementary School
Traverse City, Michigan

Blair Elementary School
Traverse City, Michigan

Bloomfield Hills Middle School
Bloomfield Hills, Michigan

Brownell Elementary School
Flint, Michigan

Catlin Gabel School
Portland, Oregon

Cherry Knoll Elementary School
Traverse City, Michigan

Cobb Middle School
Tallahassee, Florida

Courtade Elementary School
Traverse City, Michigan

Duke School for Children
Durham, North Carolina

DeVeaux Junior High School
Toledo, Ohio

East Junior High School
Traverse City, Michigan

Eastern Elementary School
Traverse City, Michigan

Eastlake Elementary School
Chula Vista, California

Eastwood Elementary School
Sturgis, Michigan

Elizabeth City Middle School
Elizabeth City, North Carolina

Franklinton Elementary School
Franklinton, North Carolina

Frick International Studies Academy
Pittsburgh, Pennsylvania

Gundry Elementary School
Flint, Michigan

Hawkins Elementary School
Toledo, Ohio

Hilltop Middle School
Chula Vista, California

Holmes Middle School
Flint, Michigan

Interlochen Elementary School
Traverse City, Michigan

Los Altos Elementary School
San Diego, California

Louis Armstrong Middle School
East Elmhurst, New York

McTigue Junior High School
Toledo, Ohio

National City Middle School
National City, California

Norris Elementary School
Traverse City, Michigan

Northeast Middle School
Minneapolis, Minnesota

Oak Park Elementary School
Traverse City, Michigan

Old Mission Elementary School
Traverse City, Michigan

Old Orchard Elementary School
Toledo, Ohio

Portland Middle School
Portland, Michigan

Reizenstein Middle School
Pittsburgh, Pennsylvania

Sabin Elementary School
Traverse City, Michigan

Shepherd Middle School
Shepherd, Michigan

Sturgis Middle School
Sturgis, Michigan

Terrell Lane Middle School
Louisburg, North Carolina

Tierra del Sol Middle School
Lakeside, California

Traverse Heights Elementary School
Traverse City, Michigan

University Preparatory Academy
Seattle, Washington

Washington Middle School
Vista, California

Waverly East Intermediate School
Lansing, Michigan

Waverly Middle School
Lansing, Michigan

West Junior High School
Traverse City, Michigan

Willow Hill Elementary School
Traverse City, Michigan

Contents

Covering and Surrounding

Pizza parlors often describe their selections as 9-inch, 12-inch, 15-inch, or even 24-inch pizzas. What do these measurements tell you about pizza size? How does the size of a pizza relate to its price? Does a 24-inch pizza generally cost twice as much as a 12-inch pizza? Should price relate to size in that way?

You may know t China has the great population of country. Which coun do you think has the greatest land area? The long borders? Which state in United States is the large Which state is the smalle How do you think land are borders, and coastlines states and countries measure

Carpet is commonly sold by the square yard. How would you estimate the cost of carpet for a room in your home? Base molding, which is used to protect the bases of walls, is usually sold by the foot. How would you estimate the cost of base molding for a room in your home?

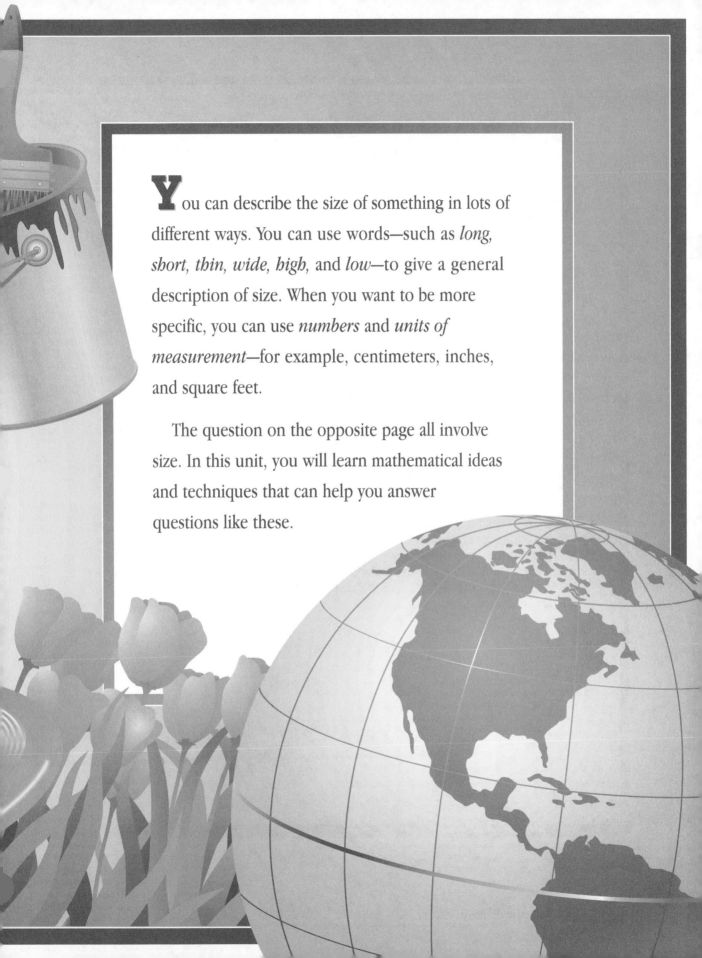

You can describe the size of something in lots of different ways. You can use words—such as *long, short, thin, wide, high,* and *low*—to give a general description of size. When you want to be more specific, you can use *numbers* and *units of measurement*—for example, centimeters, inches, and square feet.

The question on the opposite page all involve size. In this unit, you will learn mathematical ideas and techniques that can help you answer questions like these.

Mathematical Highlights

In *Covering and Surrounding*, you will explore area and perimeter of figures, in particular quadrilaterals, triangles and circles. The unit should help you to

● Understand area as a measure of *covering* a figure and perimeter as a measure of *surrounding* a figure;

● Explore whether perimeter and area are related and if so, how;

● Develop strategies for finding areas and perimeters of rectangular shapes and irregular shapes.

● Understand how the area of a rectangle is related to the area of a triangle and of a parallelogram;

● Develop formulas or procedures—stated in words and symbols—for finding areas and perimeters of rectangles, parallelograms, triangles, and circles; and

● Recognize situations in which measuring perimeter or area will answer practical questions.

As you work the problems in this unit, make it a habit to ask questions about situations involving area and perimeter. *What quantities are in the problem? How do I know which measures of a figure are involved—area or perimeter? Is an exact answer required? Is the figure an irregular or a regular shape? Is the shape made up of other shapes? What strategy or formula will help me find the area or the perimeter of the shape?*

Plan a Park

A local philanthropist, Dr. Doolittle, has just donated a piece of land to the city for a park. The plot of land is rectangular, and it measures 120 yards by 100 yards. Dr. Doolittle has also offered to donate money for construction of the park.

Dr. Doolittle wants the park to be a place that people of all ages would like to visit. She wants half of the park to be a picnic and playground area. She wants to leave the decision about what to do with the other half of the park area to someone else. She has decided to hold a design contest for the layout of the park.

Covering and Surrounding involves finding areas and perimeters of various figures and shapes. Dr. Doolittle's park design project will use the ideas you will study. After you finish the investigations in this unit, you will create a design for the park, including a scale drawing and a report that gives the dimensions of all the items you have included in your park.

As you work through each investigation, think about how you might use what you are learning to help you with your project. In particular, think about these things:

- How much space is needed for a swing set or a slide? You will need to measure one in a park or school yard near you so that your design is realistic.

- How big are tennis courts or basketball courts? You will need to find out their dimensions if you choose to put them into your park design.

- If you put in tennis courts or basketball courts, will you want a fence around them? You will need to answer this question to complete your design.

Measuring Perimeter and Area

Most Americans enjoy the rides at amusement parks and carnivals—from merry-go-rounds and Ferris wheels to roller coasters and bumper cars.

Let's suppose that a company called Midway Amusement Rides—MARs for short—builds and operates a variety of rides for amusement parks and carnivals. To do well in their business, MARs has to apply some mathematical thinking.

1.1 Designing Bumper-Car Rides

MARs sells many of its rides to traveling shows that set up their carnivals in parking lots of shopping centers and in community parks. Because they must be easy to take apart and transport, rides for traveling shows must be smaller than rides found in large amusement parks.

Bumper cars are one of the most popular rides in traveling shows. A bumper-car ride includes the cars and a smooth floor with bumper rails around it. MARs makes their bumper-car floors from tiles that are 1 meter by 1 meter squares. The bumper rail is built from sections that are 1 meter long.

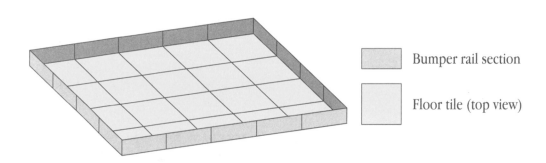

Bumper rail section

Floor tile (top view)

When MARs gets an order for a bumper-car ride, their designers sometimes use square tiles to model the possible floor plans, and then send sketches of their ideas to the customer for approval.

Problem 1.1

Solve these design problems by experimenting with square tiles.

A. Badger State Shows in Wisconsin requested a bumper-car ride with a total of 36 square meters of floor space and 26 rail sections. Sketch some possible designs for this floor plan.

B. Lone Star Carnivals in Texas wants a bumper-car ride that covers 36 square meters of floor space and has lots of rail sections for riders to bump against. Sketch some possible designs for this floor plan.

C. Design a bumper-car floor plan with 36 or more square meters of floor space that you think would make an interesting ride. Be prepared to share your design with the class and to explain why you like it.

■ Problem 1.1 Follow-Up

Two measures tell you important facts about the size of the bumper-car floor plans you have designed. The number of tiles needed to *cover* the floor is the **area** of the shape. The number of bumper rail sections needed to *surround* the floor is the **perimeter** of the shape.

1. Find the perimeter and area of each bumper-car floor plan you designed in Problem 1.1.

2. Which measure—perimeter or area—better indicates the size of a bumper-car floor plan?

The MARs company advertises its carnival rides in a catalog. One section of the catalog shows bumper-car floor plans. The catalog shows only outlines of the plans, not the grid of the floor tiles or the rail sections. Below are three of the designs shown in the catalog.

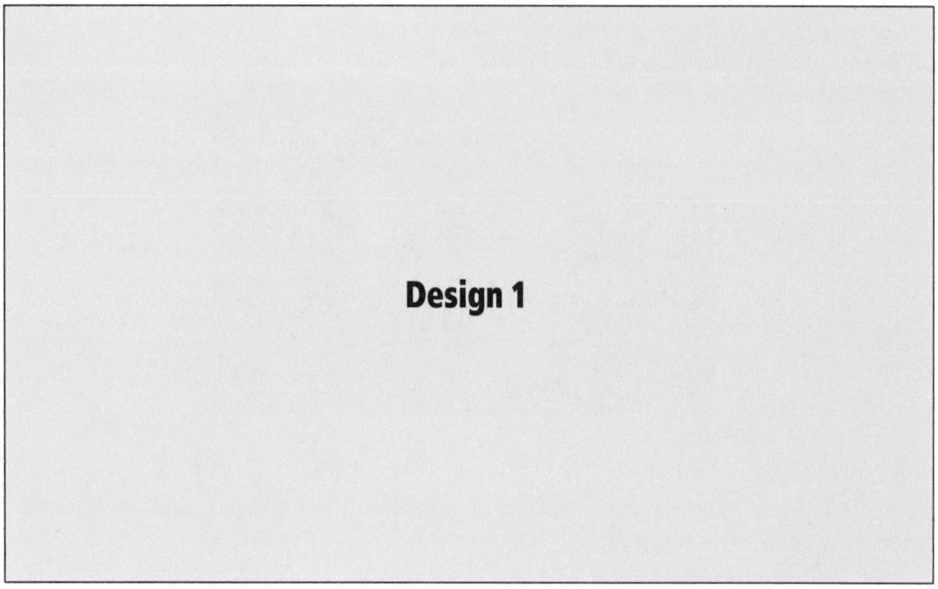

Design 1

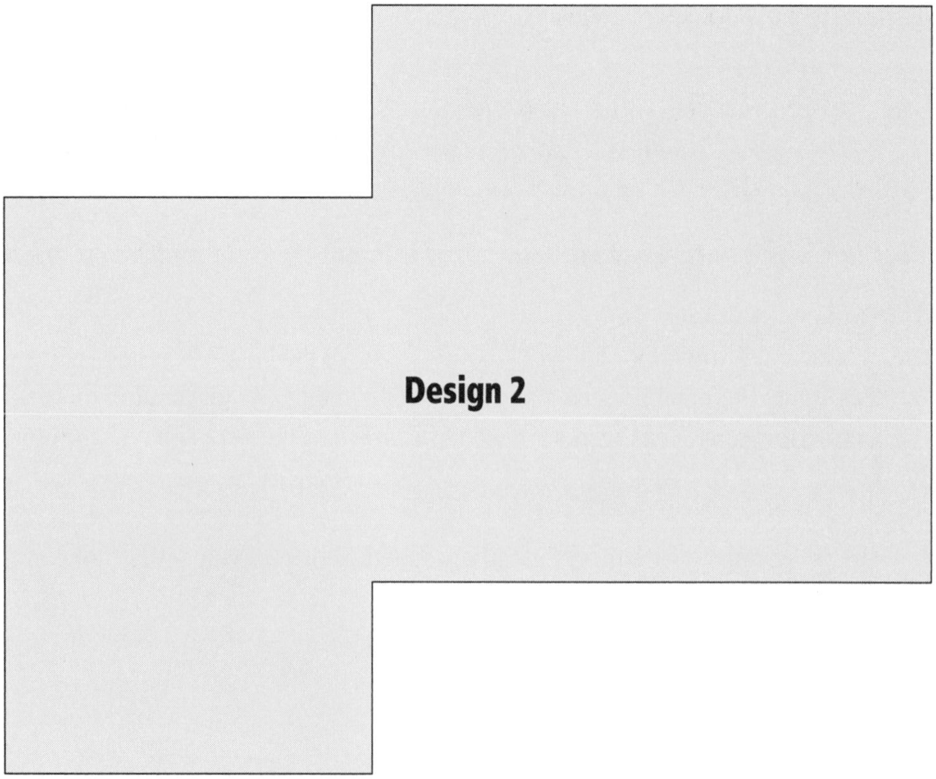

Design 2

Design 3

Problem 1.2

Use the sample rail section and floor tile below to answer these questions.

A. Which of the three designs provides the greatest floor space (has the greatest area)?

B. Which of the three designs requires the most rail sections (has the greatest perimeter)?

Sample rail section   Sample floor tile section

▪ Problem 1.2 Follow-Up

Choose the design you think is best, and explain how you would sell it to a customer.

1.3 Computing Costs

The designers at MARs specialize in creating unusual floor plans for bumper-car rides. But when it comes time to prepare estimates or bills for customers, they turn the plans over to the billing department.

The Buckeye Amusements company in Ohio wants some sample designs and cost estimates for small bumper-car rides designed for children in small cars. The MARs designers came up with the floor plans below.

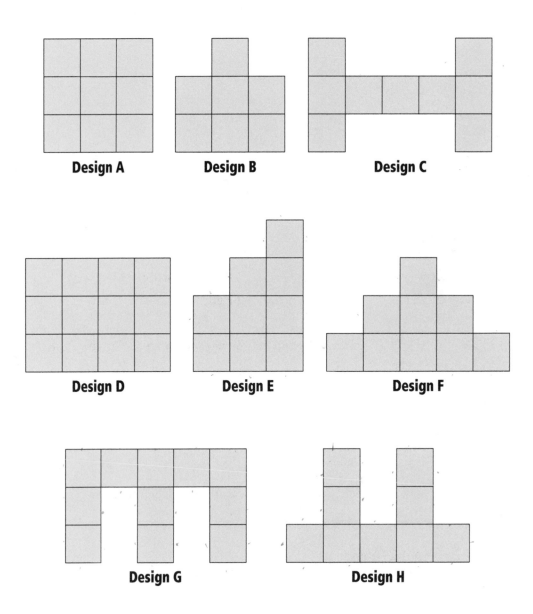

Design A

Design B

Design C

Design D

Design E

Design F

Design G

Design H

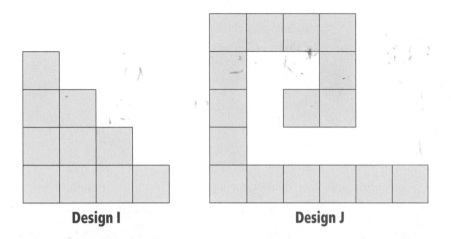

Design I   **Design J**

Problem 1.3

A. The MARs company charges $25 for each rail section and $30 for each floor tile. How much would each of the designs above cost? Record your data in a table with these column headings:

Design	Area	Perimeter	Cost of tiles	Cost of rail sections	Total cost

B. If you were the buyer for Buckeye Amusements, which design would you choose? Explain your choice.

■ **Problem 1.3 Follow-Up**

1. Of the designs above, which have an area of 9 square meters?

2. Give the price of each design you listed in question 1.

3. What accounts for the difference in the prices of the designs you listed in question 1?

1.4 Getting Your Money's Worth

Five of the bumper-car designs in Problem 1.3 had an area of 9 square meters. You found that these designs had different prices because their perimeters were different.

Problem 1.4

Questions A–E refer to the designs from Problem 1.3. Experiment with your tiles to try to answer the questions. Make sketches of your designs.

A. Build a design with the same area as design G, but with a smaller perimeter. Can you make more than one design that meets these requirements? Explain.

B. Design E can be made from design D by removing three tiles. How does the area of design D compare to the area of design E? How does the perimeter of design D compare to the perimeter of design E?

C. Design F and design I have the same perimeter. Can you rearrange the tiles of design F to make design I? Explain.

D. Design A and design C have the same area. Can you rearrange the tiles of design A to make design C? Explain.

E. Arrange your tiles to match design B. Now, move one tile to make a new design with a perimeter of 14 units. Sketch your new design.

■ Problem 1.4 Follow-Up

If two tile designs have the same area and the same perimeter, must they look exactly alike? Make a sketch to help explain your answer.

As you work on these ACE questions, use your calculator whenever you need it.

Applications ACE

1. Cut out several 1-inch paper tiles. Cover this figure with your tiles. Record the area and the perimeter of the figure.

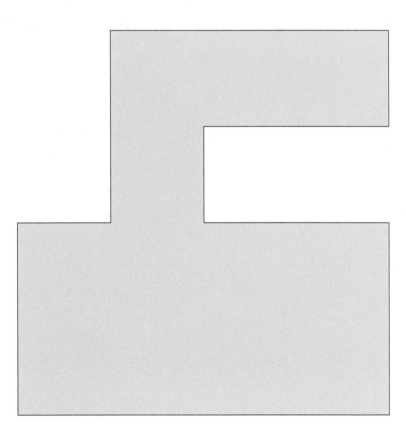

In 2–5, experiment with tiles or squares of grid paper. Sketch your final answers on grid paper.

2. Draw at least two shapes with an area of 6 square units and a perimeter of 12 units.

3. Draw at least two shapes with an area of 15 square units and a perimeter of 18 units.

4. Draw at least two shapes with an area of 12 square units and different perimeters.

5. Draw at least two shapes with a perimeter of 12 units and different areas.

In 6–9, find the area and perimeter of the shape.

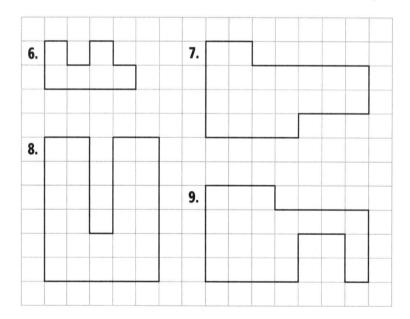

10. Look at this plan for design H.

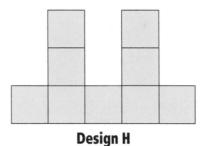

Design H

    a. If possible, design a figure with the same area as design H, but with a perimeter of 14 units. If this is not possible, explain why.

    b. If possible, design a figure with the same area as design H, but with a perimeter of 30 units. If this is not possible, explain why.

11. **a.** Copy design J onto grid paper. Add six squares to make a new design with a perimeter of 22 units.

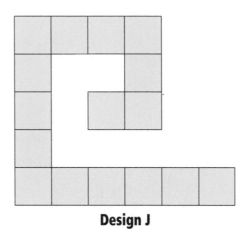

Design J

    b. Explain why the perimeters of your new design and design J are so different.

12. Carpet is commonly sold by the square yard. Base molding is commonly sold by the foot.

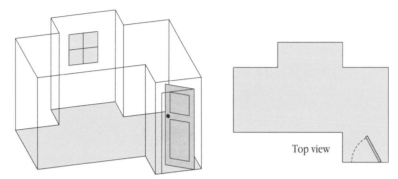

Top view

a. Describe a method you could use to *estimate* the cost of carpet for the room sketched here.

b. Describe a method you could use to *estimate* the cost of installing base molding around the base of the walls of this room.

Connections

13. Write a Logo program that will draw a rectangle with a perimeter of 200 turtle steps. Then, write a Logo program that will draw a *different* rectangle with a perimeter of 200 turtle steps.

You can describe the size and shape of a rectangle with just two numbers, *length* and *width*. In 14–16, sketch a rectangle on grid paper with the given area and with length and width that are whole numbers. Label each rectangle with its length and width.

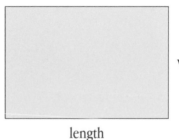

width

length

14. 18 square units

15. 20 square units

16. 23 square units

Extensions

In 17 and 18, experiment with tiles or squares of grid paper, then sketch your answers on grid paper.

17. Draw at least two shapes with a perimeter of 18 units but with different areas. Give the area of each shape.

18. Draw at least two shapes with an area of 25 square units but with different perimeters. Give the perimeter of each shape.

19. The figures drawn on the grid below are not made up entirely of whole squares.

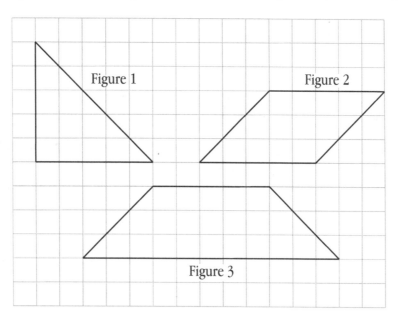

a. How would you find the area and perimeter of each figure?

b. For each figure, try your method, and record your estimates for area and perimeter.

Mathematical Reflections

In this investigation, you examined the areas and perimeters of figures made from square tiles. You found that some arrangements of tiles have large perimeters and some arrangements have smaller perimeters. These questions will help you summarize what you have learned:

1 Is it possible for two shapes to have the same area but different perimeters? Explain your answer by using words and drawings.

2 Is it possible for two shapes to have the same perimeter but different areas? Explain your answer by using words and drawings.

3 Can you figure out the perimeter of a figure if you know its area? Why or why not?

Think about your answers to these questions, discuss your ideas with other students and your teacher, and then write a summary of your findings in your journal.

At the end of this unit, you will be designing the layout for a city park. Start thinking now about what things you should consider as you create your layout. How could you apply what you know about area and perimeter to your park design?

Measuring Odd Shapes

It's not hard to find areas and perimeters of shapes made of complete squares. But measuring areas and perimeters of more interesting figures is not always easy.

2.1 Making the Shoe Fit

The clothes people wear come in many shapes and sizes. Shoes, for instance, are manufactured in thousands of types and styles. To make shoes that fit comfortably, shoe companies must know a lot about human feet.

In this problem, you will look at measures of feet and think about what measures a shoe company would need to know.

Did you know?

Although shoes are important to protect feet, for many people, they are also a fashion statement. In the 1300s, it was considered fashionable for European men to wear shoes with extremely long toes. On some of these shoes, called *crackowes*, the toe was so long that it had to be fastened to the knee with a chain so that the wearer would not trip. In the 1970s, *platform shoes,* with very thick soles, were popular. What shoe styles are popular today?

Problem 2.1

With your group, have a discussion about measuring feet. In what ways can you measure a foot? Which of these measurements would be of interest to shoe companies?

Have each person in your group trace one foot on a piece of grid paper.

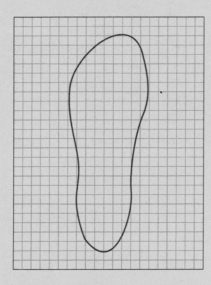

For each person's foot, estimate the length, width, area, perimeter, and any other measures your group thinks should be included. Record your data in a table with these column headings:

Student	Shoe size	Foot length	Foot width	Foot area	Foot perimeter

■ Problem 2.1 Follow-Up

Use the data from the whole class to answer these questions.

1. Does each of the data items seem reasonable? If there are outliers, do they indicate mistakes, or interesting feet?

2. a. What are the typical length, width, perimeter, and area of feet for students in your class?

   b. Explain how you organized the data and what measure(s) of center you used to decide what is typical.

3. Explain any patterns you see that would help you to predict shoe size from a particular foot measurement.

As you work on these ACE questions, use your calculator whenever you need it.

Applications

1. Below is a tracing of a student's hand on centimeter grid paper. The drawing has been reduced.

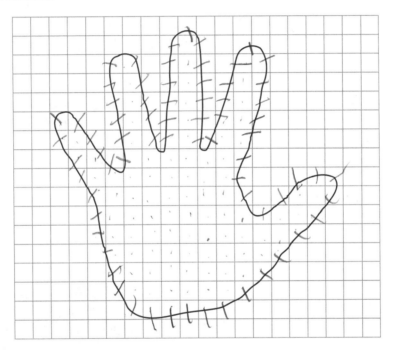

a. Estimate the area of the student's hand.

b. Use a piece of string or another method that makes sense to you to estimate the perimeter of the student's hand.

c. Explain how a company that makes gloves might be interested in area and perimeter of hands.

d. If the student's hand had been traced on half-centimeter grid paper, would your estimates be more precise, the same, or less precise? Explain.

In 2–7, use the map below. The Parks and Recreation Department bought a piece of property with two large lakes. Park planners proposed that one lake be used for swimming, fishing, and boating. The other lake would be a nature preserve with only hiking, tent camping, and canoes allowed.

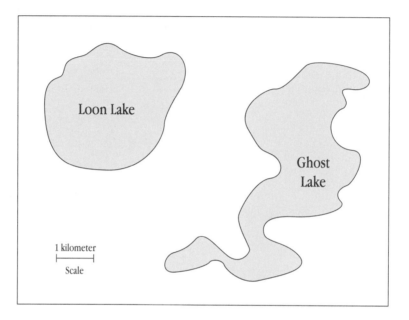

Loon Lake

Ghost Lake

1 kilometer
Scale

2. Naturalists claim that water birds need long shorelines for nesting and fishing. Which lake best meets this requirement? Explain your answer.

3. Boaters want a lake with a large area to give them space to cruise. Which lake best meets this requirement? Explain your answer.

4. Which lake has space for the greatest number of lakeside campsites? Explain your answer.

5. People who race powerboats like long stretches of water without turns. Which lake best meets this requirement? Explain your answer.

6. Sailors like lakes with long stretches to enable them to sail with any wind direction. Which lake best meets this requirement? Explain your answer.

7. Which lake do you think would be best to use for swimming, boating, and fishing, and which would be best for the nature preserve? Prepare an argument defending your choices.

Connections

8. The table below gives data on measures of head circumference (the distance around the head) and waist circumference (the distance around the waist) for 20 students.

Student	Head circumference (inches)	Waist circumference (inches)
M.S.	21.5	29.5
C.A.	23.5	32
P.B.	22	27.5
G.L.	23.25	26
K.B.	23	38.5
S.M.	21.5	23.5
K.E.	22.5	29.5
B.D.	23	27
J.G.	21	27
P.N.	21.5	28.5
L.C.	23	28
J.Y.	22	25
R.M.	21	26
J.H.	21.5	25
M.N.	23.5	25.5
M.L.	20.5	23
W.S.	20.5	31
J.J.	22	22
B.A.	23.5	31
C.F.	22.5	35

a. Make a coordinate graph with waist circumference on the horizontal axis and head circumference on the vertical axis.

b. Do you think there is a relationship between head circumference and waist circumference? Why or why not?

c. What would be a good estimate for the head circumference of a student with a waist circumference of 30 inches?

d. What would be a good estimate for the waist circumference of a student with a head circumference of 24 inches?

In 9–12, explain how perimeter is related to the size of each item.

9. Belts

10. Jeans

11. Hats

12. Shirts

In 13–15, explain how area or perimeter (or both) would be useful for the activity.

13. Painting a room or an entire house

14. Designing a parking lot

15. Designing a school playground surrounded by a fence

Extensions

16. Find a map of your city or state. Use the map's scale to estimate the area and the length of the border of your city or state.

In 17–21, use a world atlas or an encyclopedia to answer the question.

17. What is the world's longest river? What type of measurement was used to determine that it is the longest?

18. What is the world's largest lake? What type of measurement was used to determine that it is the largest?

19. Which country is the largest in the world? What type of measurement was used to determine that it is the largest?

20. What is the world's tallest mountain? What type of measurement was used to determine that it is the tallest?

21. What is the world's largest island? What type of measurement was used to determine that it is the largest?

In 22 and 23, use this map of Lake Okeehele and a centimeter grid transparency.

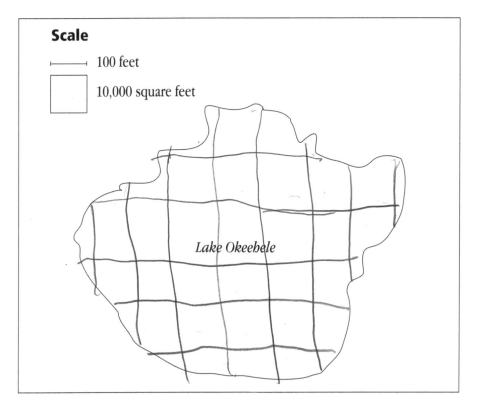

Scale

⊢———⊣ 100 feet

☐ 10,000 square feet

Lake Okeehele

22. A developer plans to build houses around Lake Okeehele. If most of his customers want to buy about 100 feet of lakefront, how many lots can the developer build around the lake? Explain your answer.

23. The buyers want to know whether the lake has shrunk or grown over time. The developer found in the county records that the lake covered 500,000 square feet in 1920. What is happening to the lake? Give evidence to support your answer.

24. The state of Hawaii is a group of islands. Atlases and almanacs report the area of Hawaii as 6450 square miles and the shoreline as 1052 miles. How do you think these measurements were made? You might want to ask your geography teacher for more information.

Did you know?

The islands of Hawaii were formed from the eruptions of many volcanoes over tens of thousands of years. Volcanoes in the island chain are still erupting today—both above and below the water. Volcanoes continually add new land to Hawaii, so the area and perimeter of the state are increasing. Someday the buildup of hardened volcanic matter under the ocean will emerge as a new Hawaiian island.

Mathematical Reflections

In this investigation, you examined areas and perimeters of odd shapes using square grids and grid paper. These questions will help you summarize what you have learned:

1 Describe how you can find the area and perimeter of an odd shape such as a footprint.

2 If two odd shapes have the same perimeter, do they have the same area?

3 Can you figure out the perimeter of an odd shape if you know its area? Why or why not?

Think about your answers to these questions, discuss your ideas with other students and your teacher, and then write a summary of your findings in your journal.

What objects in a park might have odd shapes—a flower garden? A picnic area? A play area?

Constant Area, Changing Perimeter

In making floor plans for anything from a doghouse to a dream house, you have many options. Even when area and perimeter are fixed, there are lots of possible floor plans. Many factors—including the cost of materials and the purposes of the rooms—help to determine the best possible plan.

3.1 Building Storm Shelters

From March 12–14, 1993, a fierce winter storm hit the eastern United States from Florida to Maine. Thousands of people were stranded in the snow, far from shelter. A group of 24 Michigan students, who had been hiking in the Smoky Mountains of Tennessee, were among those stranded.

To prepare for this kind of emergency, parks often provide shelters at points along major hiking trails. Since the shelters are only for emergency use, they are designed to be simple and inexpensive buildings that are easily maintained.

Problem 3.1

The rangers in Great Smoky Mountains National Park want to build several inexpensive storm shelters. The shelters must have 24 square meters of floor space. Suppose that the walls are made of sections that are 1 meter wide and cost $125.

A. Use your tiles to experiment with different rectangular shapes. Sketch each possible floor plan on grid paper. Record your group's data in a table with these column headings:

Length   Width   Perimeter   Area   Cost of walls

B. Based on the cost of the wall sections, which design would be the least expensive to build? Describe what that shelter would look like.

C. Which shelter plan has the most expensive set of wall sections? Describe what that shelter would look like.

▣ Problem 3.1 Follow-Up

Can you find a design—other than a rectangle—with 24 square meters of floor space and lower wall-section costs than any of the designs you have looked at so far? Experiment with your tiles to answer this question.

3.2 Stretching the Perimeter

In Problem 3.1, you worked with rectangles to help you understand the relationship between area and perimeter. In this problem, you will look at what happens when you cut an interesting part from a rectangle and slide that piece onto another edge. Look at these examples:

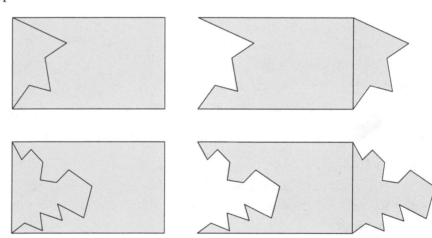

Can you use this technique to find a nonrectangular shape with an area of 24 square units and a larger perimeter than any of the rectangles you've found?

Problem 3.2

Draw a 4×6 rectangle on grid paper, and cut it out.

Starting at one corner, cut an interesting path to an adjacent corner.

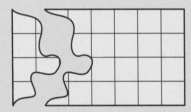

Slide the piece you cut out onto the opposite edge. Tape the two pieces together, matching the straight edges.

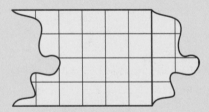

A. Find the area and the perimeter of your new figure.

B. Is the perimeter of the new figure larger than, the same as, or smaller than the perimeter of a 4×6 rectangle? Explain.

C. Could you make a figure with an area of 24 square units with a longer perimeter than you found in your first figure? Explain your answer.

■ Problem 3.2 Follow-Up

Summarize what you have discovered about figures with an area of 24 square units.

As you work on these ACE questions, use your calculator whenever you need it.

Applications

1. Sketch all the rectangles with an area of 30 square units and whole-number side lengths.

2. If the park rangers in Problem 3.1 wanted to build storm shelters with 20 square meters of floor space instead of 24, what design would be the least expensive?

3. Find the rectangle with an area 36 square units and whole-number side lengths that has the smallest perimeter possible.

4. Alyssa is designing a rectangular sandbox. The bottom is to cover 16 square feet. What shape will require the least amount of material for the sides of the sandbox?

5. Suppose you wanted to make a large banquet table from 36 square card tables. Four people can be seated at a card table, one person on each side. With two card tables put together to make a larger table, six people can be seated:

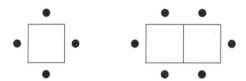

How would you arrange the 36 card tables to make the banquet table seat the greatest number of people? Explain your reasoning.

Connections

6. In a–c, find all rectangles that can be made from the given number of tiles.

   a.   60 square tiles   **b.**   61 square tiles   **c.**   62 square tiles

   d.   How can you use your work in a–c to list the factors of 60, 61, and 62?

Extensions

7. A *pentomino* is a shape made of five identical squares that are connected along straight edges.

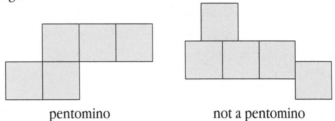

pentomino   not a pentomino

Turning or flipping a pentomino does *not* make a different pentomino.

a. Find all the possible pentominos. On grid paper, sketch each pentomino that you find.

b. Why do you think you have found all the possible pentominos?

c. Which pentomino has the smallest perimeter? Which pentomino has the largest perimeter?

8. a. On grid paper, design a 120-square-foot bedroom that you would enjoy having for your own. Draw in furniture on your floor plan. Measure real rooms, closets, and furniture to see whether your design is reasonable. Record the measurements you find. Include measures for a bed and a dresser.

b. Describe why you think your design would be a good design for a bedroom. Include how you decided what would be reasonable for the shape of the room, the size of closets, and the other features of your design.

Mathematical Reflections

In this investigation, you designed storm shelters with an area of 24 square meters and determined which design would cost the least because it had the smallest perimeter. This problem helped you see how the perimeters of rectangles made from the same number of tiles can vary. You also looked at the perimeters of nonrectangular shapes with an area of 24 square units. These questions will help you summarize what you have learned:

1 If two rectangles have the same area, must they also have the same perimeter? Explain your answer.

2 Of all possible rectangles with a given area and whole-number side lengths, which has the smallest perimeter?

3 Of all possible rectangles with a given area and whole-number side lengths, which has the largest perimeter?

Think about your answers to these questions, discuss your ideas with other students and your teacher, and then write a summary of your findings in your journal.

Think about the city park you will be designing. You will have to use part of the area of the park for picnic tables, playground equipment, and other attractions. How could what you have learned about the relationship of perimeter and area be useful to you? You might want to visit some local parks to get more ideas for how you will design your city park. You may also want to measure some things in the parks you visit so you have a good idea about what size things in your design should be. Don't forget to record everything you find out!

Constant Perimeter, Changing Area

You often encounter situations in which you want to make the most of something. For example, suppose you were planning a party and had a set amount of money to spend on decorations and refreshments. Or, imagine that you were going on a trip and had a certain amount of spending money. In either situation, you would want to make the most of your budget.

Sometimes you want to make the least of something. If you were building a toy airplane or a racing bicycle, you would want to make it as lightweight as possible.

Mathematicians call these kinds of tasks finding the *maximum* or finding the *minimum*. In the last investigation, you found the maximum and minimum *perimeter* you could have for a rectangle with a fixed area of 24 square meters and whole-number side lengths. In this investigation, you will start with a fixed *perimeter* and try to find the maximum and minimum *area* that perimeter can enclose.

4.1 Fencing in Spaces

Americans have over 50 million dogs as pets. In many parts of the country—particularly in cities—there are laws against letting dogs run free. Many people build pens so their dogs have a chance to get outside for fresh air and exercise.

Suppose you wanted to help a friend build a rectangular pen for her dog, Shane. You have 24 meters of fencing, in 1-meter lengths, to build the pen. Which rectangular shape would be best for Shane?

Experiment with your square tiles to find all possible rectangles with a *perimeter* of 24 meters. Sketch each rectangle on grid paper. Record your data about each possible plan in a table with these column headings:

Length   Width   Perimeter   Area

■ **Problem 4.1 Follow-Up**

1. Which design would give Shane the best pen for running?

2. Which design would give Shane the most space for playing?

4.2 Adding Tiles to Pentominos

In Problem 4.1, you explored the relationship between area and perimeter by investigating the rectangles that could be made with a fixed perimeter of 24 units. In this problem, you will continue to investigate fixed perimeter by adding tiles to a pentomino.

Remember that a *pentomino* is a shape made from five identical square tiles connected along their edges. Here are some examples:

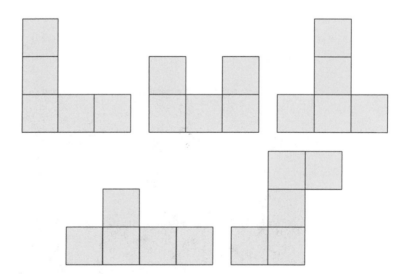

Problem 4.2

Make this pentomino with your tiles.

A. Add tiles to the pentomino to make a new figure with a perimeter of 18 units. Draw your new figure on grid paper. Show clearly where you added tiles to the pentomino.

B. What is the smallest number of tiles you can add to the pentomino to make a new figure with a perimeter of 18 units? Draw the new figure, showing where you would add tiles to the pentomino.

C. What is the largest number of tiles you can add to the pentomino to make a new figure with a perimeter of 18 units? Draw the new figure, showing where you would add tiles to the pentomino.

■ Problem 4.2 Follow-Up

How does adding one tile change the perimeter of a figure? Explain your answer. You might find it helpful to draw pictures.

As you work on these ACE questions, use your calculator whenever you need it.

Applications

1. Suneeta used square tiles to make rectangles with a perimeter of 8 units. On grid paper, draw all the possible rectangles Suneeta might have made.

2. Find a rectangle with whole-number side lengths, a perimeter of 20 units, and the largest possible area.

3. If you have 72 centimeters of molding to make a frame for a painting, how should you cut the molding to give the largest possible area for the painting?

4. On the next page is a diagram of the field next to Sarah's house. Each small square represents a space that is 1 foot on each side. Sarah wants to make a garden and a play area in the field.

    a. How much fencing does Sarah need to surround the field? Explain your answer.

    b. A box of grass seed plants an area of 125 square feet. How many boxes of seed would Sarah need to seed the entire field? Explain your answer.

    c. Sarah decides she wants to include some flower and vegetable plots and a small play area (a swing set and a sandbox) in the field. On Labsheet 4.ACE, make a design for Sarah that includes these items. Give the area and the dimensions of each part of your design.

    d. How many boxes of grass seed would Sarah need to seed the design you drew for part c?

Sarah's Field

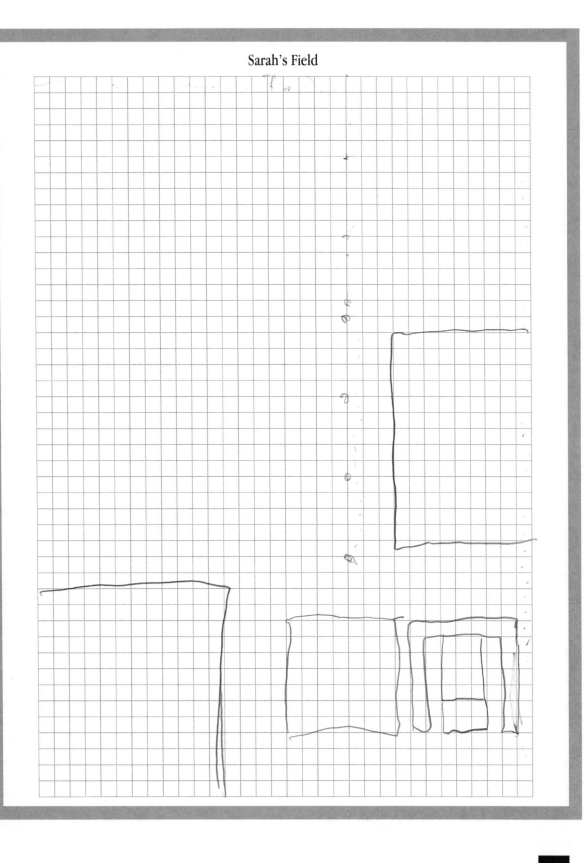

Connections

In 5–8, make any measurements you need to find the perimeter and area of the polygon in centimeters.

5.

6.

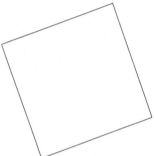

7.

8.

9. In *Shapes and Designs,* you found that if you make a rectangle out of Polystrips and press on the corners, the rectangle tilts out of a shape into a different parallelogram.

    a. How does the perimeter of the original rectangle compare to the perimeter of the new parallelogram?

    b. How does the area of the original rectangle compare to the area of the new parallelogram?

10. Kate and Eli want to design a garage with an area of 240 square feet.

    a. Make an organized list showing the dimensions (length and width), in feet, of all the possible rectangular garages they could make with whole-number dimensions.

    b. Which rectangles would be reasonable for a garage? Explain your answer.

    c. Which rectangle would you choose for a garage? Why?

11. **a.** Find the perimeter and area of the rectangle below.

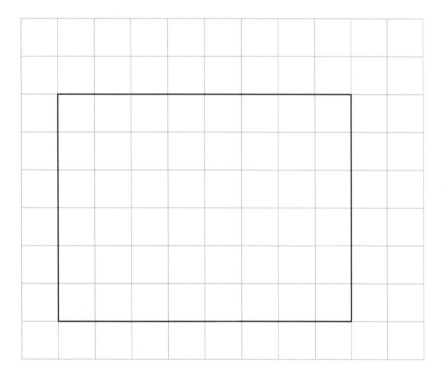

= 1 square meter

b. On grid paper, draw a rectangle with the same area as the one shown on the previous page, but a different perimeter. Label its dimensions, and give its perimeter.

c. On your grid paper, draw a rectangle with the same perimeter as the rectangle you just drew, but a different area. Label its dimensions, and give its area.

In 12 and 13, give the area, in square inches, and the perimeter, in inches, of the rectangle.

12.

13.

14. a. Find the area and perimeter of the rectangle below.

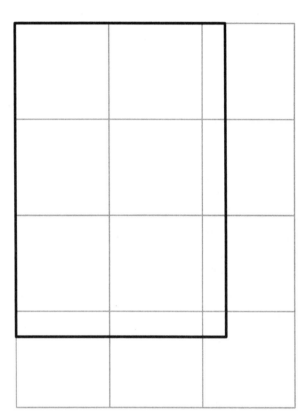

b. On inch grid paper, draw a rectangle with the same perimeter as the rectangle shown, but with a different area. Label the rectangle with its length and width, and give its area.

Extensions

15. Suppose a square sheet of paper has a perimeter of 1 meter.

    a. What is the length of each side?

    b. Suppose you folded the square sheet in half. What new shape would you have? What would the lengths of the shape's four sides be? What would the perimeter be?

    c. Suppose you had folded over the top $\frac{1}{4}$ of the square. What new shape would you have? What would the lengths of the shape's four sides be? What would the perimeter be?

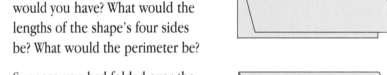

    d. Suppose you had folded over only the top $\frac{1}{8}$ of the square. What new shape would you have? What would the lengths of the shape's four sides be? What would the perimeter be?

    e. What would you predict for the perimeter of the shape you would get by folding over $\frac{1}{16}$ of the square?

Mathematical Reflections

In this investigation, you examined how the areas of shapes with the same perimeter could vary. First, you looked at rectangular pens with perimeters of 24 meters and decided which pens would give a dog the most room for running and for playing. Then you experimented with adding tiles to a pentomino, and you determined the smallest and the largest numbers of tiles you could add to the pentomino to make a shape with a perimeter of 18 units. These questions will help you summarize what you have learned:

1 Do all rectangles with the same perimeter have the same area? Explain your answer.

2 Of all rectangles with a given perimeter and whole-number side lengths, which rectangle has the smallest area?

3 Of all rectangles with a given perimeter and whole-number side lengths, which rectangle has the largest area?

Think about your answers to these questions, discuss your ideas with other students and your teacher, and then write a summary of your findings in your journal.

When you design the city park, how will these new ideas about perimeter and area help you? What things in a park would require information about area and perimeter? What areas might you want fencing around? Will you have sidewalks or paths in your park? You might want to start measuring some things like sidewalks and basketball courts now in preparation for designing the park. Remember to record in your journal all measurements that might help you with your project.

Measuring Parallelograms

You have found areas and perimeters of both rectangular and nonrectangular shapes. When a rectangle is displayed on a grid, you can find the area by counting the number of squares enclosed by the rectangle. You may have found that, once you counted the grid squares in one row, you could multiply by the number of rows to find the total number of squares in the rectangle. In other words, you can find the area of a rectangle by multiplying the length by the width.

For example, in this rectangle there are 5 squares in the first row and 7 rows in all. The area of the rectangle is $5 \times 7 = 35$ square units.

For a nonrectangular figure, you found that you could estimate the area by covering the figure with a grid and counting square units. In the next two investigations, you will find shortcuts for calculating areas of some special figures, including parallelograms. But don't forget that you can always cover a figure with a grid and count squares to find area.

5.1 Finding Measures of Parallelograms

On the next page are seven parallelograms drawn on a grid. Some of the parallelograms are not covered by whole squares. Even the two rectangles have sides that are not whole numbers of units long.

Problem 5.1

For parallelograms A–G, find the area and explain how you found it.

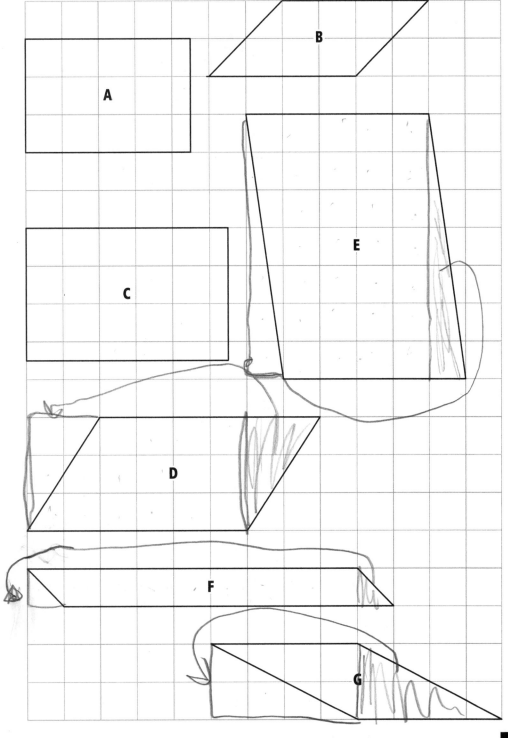

Find the area and the perimeter of this parallelogram. Explain your reasoning.

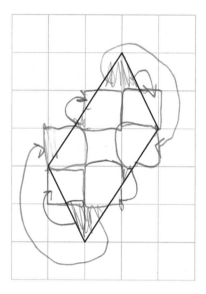

5.2 Designing Parallelograms Under Constraints

Parallelograms are often described by giving their **base** and **height.** The drawings illustrate the meanings of these terms.

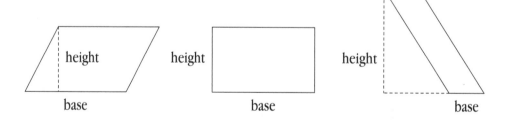

You can think of the height as the distance a rock would fall if you dropped it from a point at the top of a parallelogram down to the line that the base is on. In the first parallelogram, if we dropped the rock from the upper-left corner, it would fall inside the parallelogram. In the second parallelogram (a rectangle), the rock could fall along one of the sides. In the third parallelogram, if we dropped the rock from the upper-left corner, it would fall outside the parallelogram.

In the next problem, you will draw parallelograms that meet given requirements, or *constraints*. Sometimes you will be able to draw more than one parallelogram that satisfies the constraints.

Problem 5.2

In A–E, make your drawings on centimeter grid paper. Note that cm is the abbreviation for centimeters, and cm^2 is the abbreviation for square centimeters.

A. Draw a rectangle with an area of 18 cm^2. Then, try to draw a different rectangle with an area of 18 cm^2. Do the rectangles have the same perimeter? If you couldn't draw a different rectangle, explain why.

B. Draw a rectangle with the dimensions 3 cm by 8 cm. Then, try to draw a different rectangle with these same dimensions. Do the rectangles have the same area? If you couldn't draw a different rectangle, explain why.

C. Draw a parallelogram with a base of 7 cm and a height of 4 cm. Then, try to draw a different parallelogram with these same dimensions. Do the parallelograms have the same area? If you couldn't draw a different parallelogram, explain why.

D. Draw a parallelogram with all side lengths equal to 6 cm. Then, try to draw a different parallelogram with all side lengths equal to 6 cm. Do the parallelograms have the same area? If you couldn't draw a different parallelogram, explain why.

E. Draw a parallelogram with an area of 30 cm^2. Then, try to draw a different parallelogram with the same area. Do the parallelograms have the same perimeter? If you couldn't draw a different parallelogram, explain why.

Problem 5.2 Follow-Up

1. Summarize what you have discovered from making parallelograms that fit given constraints. Include your feelings about what kinds of constraints make designing a parallelogram easy and what kinds of constraints make designing a parallelogram difficult.

2. Have you discovered any shortcuts for finding areas of parallelograms? If so, describe them.

5.3 Rearranging Parallelograms

As you have probably discovered in your work, it would be useful to develop some easy ways to find perimeters and areas of common polygons without having to cover them with a grid and count squares. Let's do some exploring...

Problem 5.3

Draw two different nonrectangular parallelograms on a sheet of grid paper, and cut them out. Cut one of your parallelograms into two pieces so that the pieces can be reassembled to form a rectangle. Do the same for the second parallelogram. Use one of your parallelograms to complete parts A–C.

A. Record the base, height, perimeter, and area of the original parallelogram.

B. Record the length, width, perimeter, and area of the rectangle you made from the parallelogram pieces.

C. What relationships do you see between the measures for the rectangle and the measures for the parallelogram from which it was made?

■ Problem 5.3 Follow-Up

Use what you have learned to find the area and perimeter of this parallelogram.

As you work on these ACE questions, use your calculator whenever you need it.

Applications

In 1–7, find the area and perimeter of the polygon, and write a brief explanation of your reasoning for 2, 6, and 7.

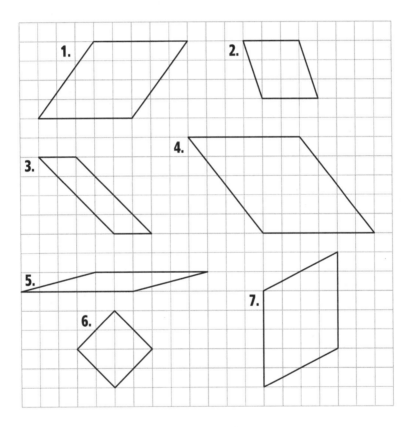

8. Below is a *family* of parallelograms.

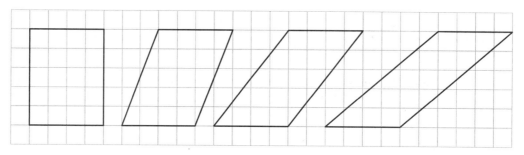

   a. Find the area of each parallelogram.

   b. What patterns do you see?

   c. Why do you think these parallelograms are called a family?

In 9–11, find the perimeter and area of the parallelogram.

9.

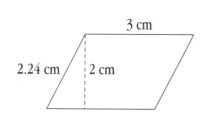

3 cm

2.24 cm   2 cm

10.

6 cm

1 cm

2.24 cm

11.

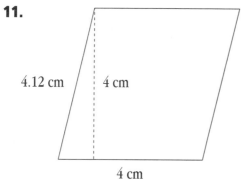

4.12 cm   4 cm

4 cm

Connections

12. In *Shapes and Designs*, you found that if you make a rectangle out of Polystrips and press on the corners, the rectangle tilts out of a shape into a different parallelogram.

a. How will the sides, angles, area, and perimeter of the new parallelogram compare to the original rectangle?

b. What relations among the sides and angles of rectangles are also true of parallelograms?

13. In *Shapes and Designs*, you learned about shapes that can tile a flat surface.

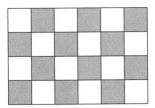  

a. The floor plan on the following page is to be tiled with rectangular tiles like the one shown. Use your understanding of area and perimeter to calculate the number of tiles needed to cover the floor. Explain your reasoning.

b. How would your reasoning change if you were to use nonrectangular parallelograms as tiles?

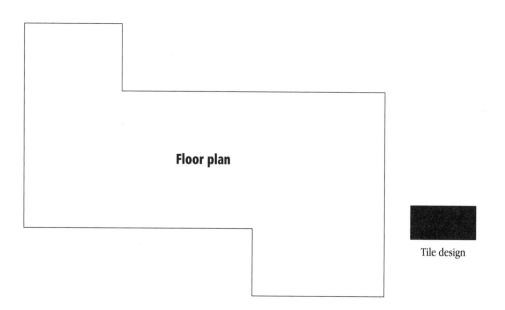

Floor plan

Tile design

14. Suppose you had a plot of land and you wanted to use what you have learned in this unit to design a garden. Design a parallelogram-shaped flower bed with an area of 24 square feet.

Extensions

15. Draw a parallelogram with a base of 6 centimeters and an area of 30 square centimeters. If possible, draw a second parallelogram with the same dimensions.

16. Design a rectangle with an area of 9 square centimeters. Make two sides a whole-number length, and two sides a length that is not a whole number. If possible, draw a second rectangle under these same constraints.

Mathematical Reflections

In this investigation, you invented strategies for finding areas and perimeters of parallelograms. These questions will help you summarize what you have learned:

1 Describe at least one efficient way to find the area of a parallelogram. Explain why it works.

2 Describe at least one efficient way to find the perimeter of a parallelogram. Explain why it works.

Think about your answers to these questions, discuss your ideas with other students and your teacher, and then write a summary of your findings in your journal.

How might your new knowledge about parallelograms help you in your park design? Have you thought about designing picnic areas or gardens in the shape of a parallelogram?

Measuring Triangles

You can always find the area of a figure by overlaying a grid and counting squares, but you probably realize that this can be very time-consuming. In Investigation 5, you discovered a shortcut for finding the area of a parallelogram without counting squares. In this investigation, you will estimate areas of triangles and look for patterns that might help you discover a shortcut for finding the area of a triangle.

6.1 Finding Measures of Triangles

On the next page are eight triangles drawn on a grid. The triangles are not covered by whole numbers of unit squares.

> ### Problem 6.1
>
> For triangles A–H on page 57, find the area and perimeter and explain how you found them.

■ **Problem 6.1 Follow-Up**

Find the area and perimeter of this triangle. Explain your reasoning.

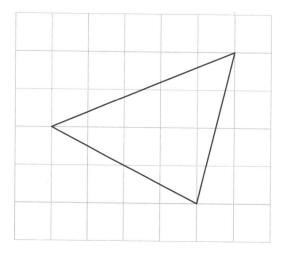

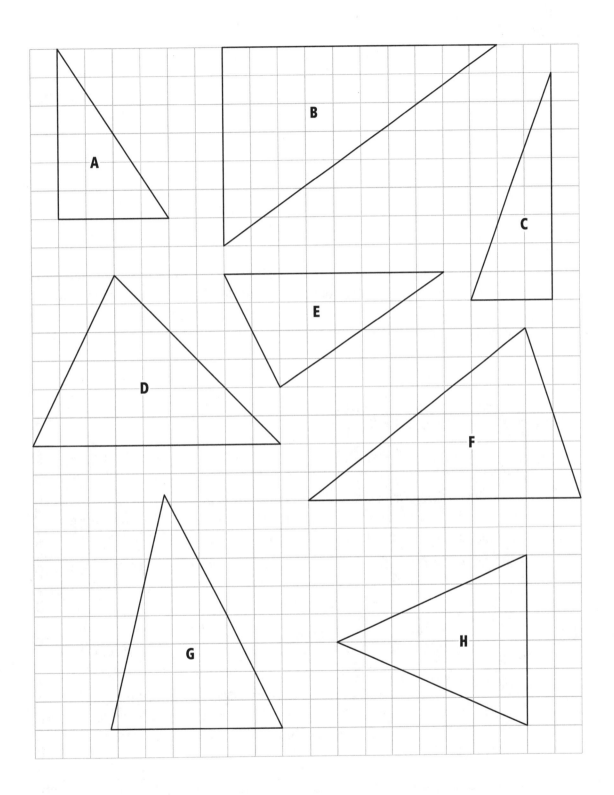

6.2 Designing Triangles Under Constraints

As with parallelograms, triangles are often described by giving their base and height. The drawings below illustrate what these terms mean.

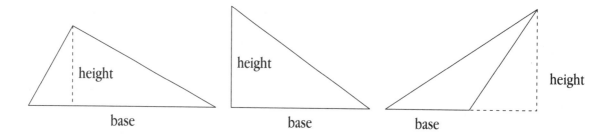

You can think of the height of a triangle as the distance a rock would fall if you dropped it from the top vertex of the triangle down to the line that the base is on. In the first triangle, the height falls inside the triangle. In the second triangle, the height is one of the sides. In the third triangle, the height falls outside the triangle.

In this problem, you will try to draw triangles that meet given constraints.

Problem 6.2

In A–D, make your drawings on centimeter grid paper. Remember that cm is the abbreviation for centimeters, and cm² is the abbreviation for square centimeters.

A. Draw a triangle with a base of 5 cm and a height of 6 cm. Then, try to draw a different triangle with these same dimensions. Do the triangles have the same area? If you couldn't draw a different triangle, explain why.

B. Draw a triangle with an area of 15 cm². Then, try to draw a different triangle with an area of 15 cm². Do the triangles have the same perimeter? If you couldn't draw a different triangle, explain why.

C. Draw a triangle with sides of length 3 cm, 4 cm, and 5 cm. Then, try to draw a different triangle with these same side lengths. Do the triangles have the same area? If you couldn't draw a different triangle, explain why.

D. A **right triangle** is a triangle that has a right angle. Draw a right triangle with a 30° angle. Then, try to draw a different right triangle with a 30° angle. Do the triangles have the same area? If you couldn't draw a different triangle, explain why.

■ Problem 6.2 Follow-Up

1. Summarize what you have discovered from making triangles that fit given constraints. Include your feelings about what kinds of constraints make designing a triangle easy and what kinds of constraints make designing a triangle difficult.

2. Have you discovered any shortcuts for finding areas of triangles? If so, describe them.

6.3 Making Parallelograms from Triangles

In *Shapes and Designs*, you discovered that triangles are useful for building because they are stable figures. If you make a triangle out of three Polystrips, you cannot "squish" it into a different shape. In this problem, you will experiment with paper triangles to try to discover a shortcut for finding the area of a triangle.

Problem 6.3

Draw two triangles on a sheet of grid paper. Make sure the triangles are very different from one another. For each triangle, complete parts A–C.

A. Record the base, height, area, and perimeter of your triangle.

B. Make a copy of your triangle, and cut out both copies. Experiment with putting the two triangles together to make new polygons. Describe and sketch the polygons that are possible.

C. Can you make a parallelogram by piecing together the two identical triangles? If so, record the base, height, area, and perimeter of the parallelogram. How do these measures compare to the measures of the original triangles?

D. Draw a parallelogram on grid paper, and cut it out. Can you cut the parallelogram into two triangles that are the same shape and size? Describe and sketch what you find.

■ Problem 6.3 Follow-Up

Use what you have learned to find the area and perimeter of this triangle.

As you work on these ACE questions, use your calculator whenever you need it.

Applications

In 1–6, calculate the area and perimeter of the polygon, and briefly explain your reasoning for figures 2, 4, and 6.

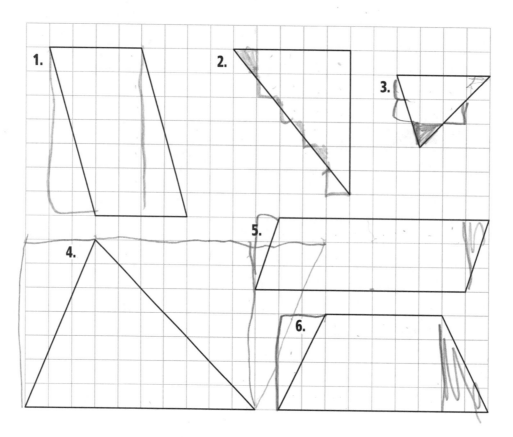

7. On the following page is a *family* of triangles.

    a. Find the area of each triangle.

    b. What patterns do you see?

    c. Why do you think these triangles are called a family?

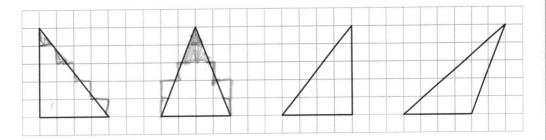

In 8–11, find the perimeter and area of the figure.

8.

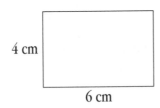

4 cm

6 cm

9.

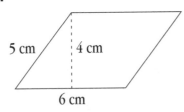

5 cm   4 cm

6 cm

10.

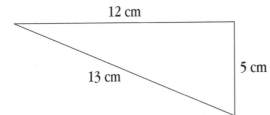

12 cm

5 cm

13 cm

11.

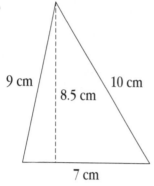

In 12–17, make whatever measurements you need to find the perimeter and area of the figure. Measure in centimeters.

12.

13.

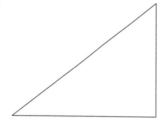

14.

15.

16.

17.

Connections

18. **a.** Explain how the base and height could be measured in these figures.

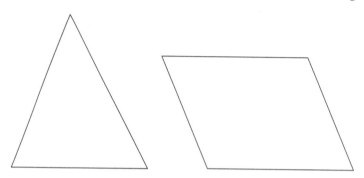

b. Explain how the base and height could be measured in this triangle.

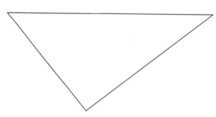

c. Explain how base and height are used to calculate area for parallelograms and triangles. Explain why this method works.

19. A **trapezoid** is a polygon with at least two opposite edges parallel. Below are two trapezoids drawn on grid paper.

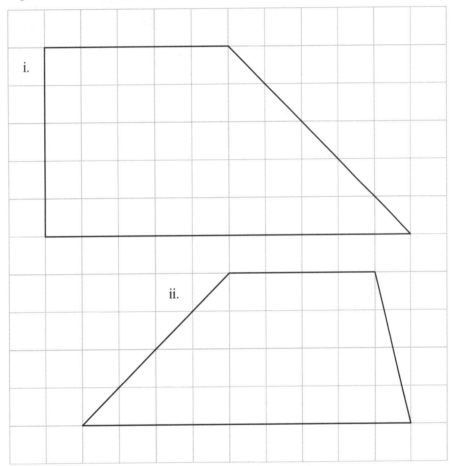

i.

ii.

a. Try to find a way to find the area of a trapezoid without having to count each square. Use your method to find the area for each trapezoid. Summarize your method as a rule or a description.

b. How can you find the perimeter of a trapezoid? Use your method to calculate the perimeter of each trapezoid. Summarize your method as a rule or a description.

Extensions

20. Explain how you could calculate the area and perimeter of this hexagon.

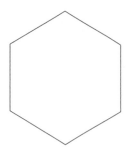

In 21 and 22, find the perimeter and area of the figure.

21.

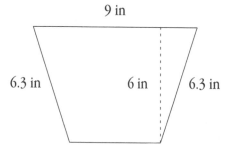

22.

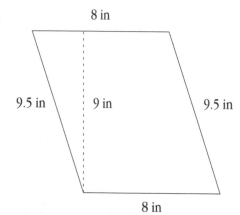

23. You saw earlier that in some parallelograms and triangles, the height falls outside of the shape being measured.

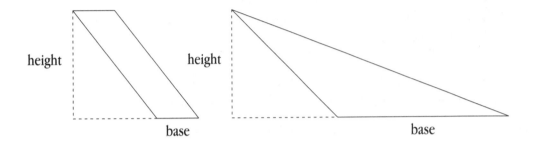

a. The area of the parallelogram can still be calculated by multiplying the base times the height. Write an explanation of why this is true.

b. The area of the triangle can still be calculated by multiplying $\frac{1}{2}$ times the base times the height. Write an explanation of why this is true.

Mathematical Reflections

In this investigation, you invented strategies for finding areas and perimeters of triangles by relating them to parallelograms and rectangles. These questions will help you summarize what you have learned:

1 Describe an efficient way to find the area of a triangle. Be sure to mention the measurements you would need to make and how you would use them to find the area.

2 Describe an efficient way to find the perimeter of a triangle. Be sure to mention the measurements you would need to make and how you would use them to find the perimeter.

3 Summarize what you have discovered about finding areas and perimeters of rectangles, parallelograms, and triangles. Describe the measures you need to make to find the area and perimeter of each figure.

Think about your answers to these questions, discuss your ideas with other students and your teacher, and then write a summary of your findings in your journal.

Are you finalizing your ideas for what you want to put in your park? Have you considered including a picnic area, a tennis court, a basketball court, a water fountain, or rest rooms? What kind of ground covering might you use for the playground area—concrete, sand, grass, wood chips? Keep track of your ideas in your journal.

Going Around in Circles

You encounter circles every day of your life. They are one of the most useful shapes. Circles are used for making things like tools, toys, and transportation vehicles, and everyday items like bottle caps, compact discs, and coins. Take a minute to think of how different your life would be without circles.

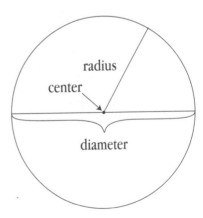

There are at least four measurements that are useful for describing the size of a **circle**: *diameter, radius, area,* and *circumference.* The **diameter** of a circle is any line segment that extends from a point on the circle, through the center, to another point on the circle. The **radius** is any line segment from the center to a point on the circle. **Circumference** means *perimeter* in the language of circles—it is the distance around the circle.

It is easy to measure the diameter and radius of a circle, but measuring the area and circumference is not as easy. You can't cover the circle with an exact number of square tiles to compute the area, and you can't easily use a ruler to measure its circumference.

As you work on the problems in this investigation, look for connections between a circle's diameter, radius, area, and circumference. Search for clues that tell when each of these measurements gives useful information about a circular object in a given situation.

7.1 Pricing Pizza

Many pizza restaurants sell small, medium, and large pizzas— usually measured by the diameter of a circular pie. Of course, the prices are different for the three sizes. Do you think a large pizza is usually the best buy?

Problem 7.1

The Sole D'Italia Pizzeria sells small, medium, and large pizzas. A small is 9 inches in diameter, a medium is 12 inches in diameter, and a large is 15 inches in diameter. Prices for cheese pizzas are $6.00 for small, $9.00 for medium, and $12.00 for large.

A. Draw a 9-inch, a 12-inch, and a 15-inch "pizza" on centimeter grid paper. Let 1 centimeter of the grid paper represent 1 inch on the pizza. Estimate the radius, circumference, and area of each pizza. (You may want to use string to help you find the circumference.)

B. Which measurement—radius, diameter, circumference, or area—seems most closely related to price? Explain your answer.

▪ Problem 7.1 Follow-Up

Use your results to write a report about what you consider to be the best value of the pizza options at Sole D'Italia.

7.2 Surrounding a Circle

Mathematicians have found a relationship between the diameter and circumference of a circle. You can try to discover this relationship by measuring many different circles and looking for patterns. The patterns you discover can help you develop a shortcut for finding the circumference of a circle.

Problem 7.2

In this problem, you will work with a collection of circular objects.

A. Use a tape measure to find the diameter and circumference of each object. Record your results in a table with these column headings:

Object   Diameter   Circumference

B. Make a coordinate graph of your data. Use the horizontal axis for diameter and the vertical axis for circumference.

C. Study your table and your graph, looking for patterns and relationships that will allow you to predict the circumference from the diameter. Test your ideas on some other circular objects. Once you think you have found a pattern, answer this question: What do you think the relationship is between the diameter and the circumference of a circle?

■ Problem 7.2 Follow-Up

1. How can you find the circumference of a circle if you know its diameter?

2. How can you find the diameter of the circle if you know its circumference?

3. Use the relationships you discovered in the problem to calculate the circumferences of the pizzas from Problem 7.1. How do your calculations compare to your estimates?

7.3 Covering a Circle

In the last problem, you discovered a pattern for finding the circumference of a circle. Do you think there is a similar pattern for finding the area of a circle?

Problem 7.3

Find as many different ways as you can to estimate the area of the circle below. For each method, give your area estimate and carefully describe how you found it. Include drawings in your descriptions if they help show what you did.

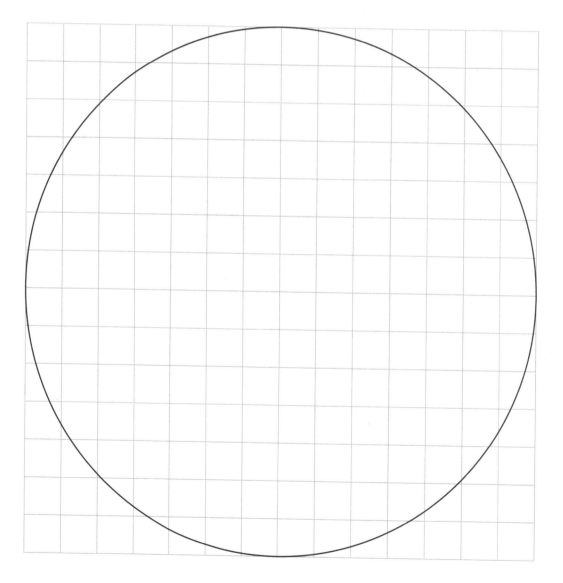

Will a circle with a diameter equal to half the diameter of the circle in the problem have an area equal to half the area of that circle? Why or why not?

7.4 "Squaring" a Circle

In Investigations 5 and 6, you learned some things about parallelograms and triangles by comparing them to rectangles. Now you will find out more about circles by comparing them to squares.

Labsheet 7.4 shows the three circles that are drawn below. A portion of each circle is covered by a shaded square. The sides of each shaded square are the same length as the radius of the circle. We call such a square a "radius square."

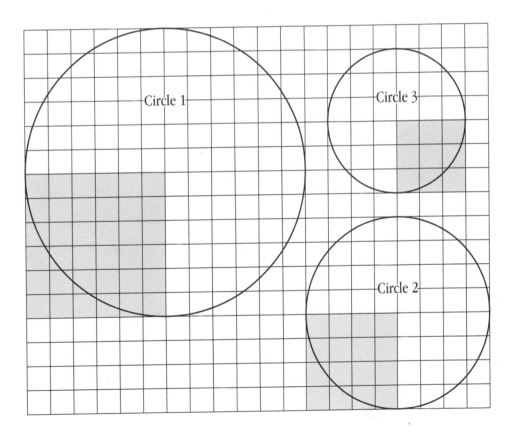

Problem 7.4

A. For each circle, cut out several copies of the radius square from a sheet of centimeter grid paper. Find out how many radius squares it takes to cover the circle. You may cut the radius squares into parts if you need to. Record your data in a table with these column headings:

Circle	Radius of circle	Area of radius square	Area of circle	Number of radius squares needed

B. Now draw a couple of your own circles on grid paper. You can use circles from the objects you measured in Problem 7.2 and from your Shapes Set. Make radius squares for each circle, and find out how many radius squares it takes to cover each circle. Add this data to your table.

C. Describe any patterns you see in your data.

D. If you were asked to estimate the area of any circle in "radius squares," what would you report as the best estimate?

Problem 7.4 Follow-Up

1. How can you find the area of a circle if you know the diameter or the radius?

2. How can you find the diameter or radius of a circle if you know the area?

Did you know?

You have discovered that the area of a circle is a *little more than 3* times the radius squared. You have also found that the distance around a circle is a *little more than 3* times the diameter. There is a special name given to this number that is a little more than 3.

In 1706, William Jones used π (pronounced "pi"), the Greek letter for *p*, to represent this number. He used the symbol to stand for the *periphery*, or distance around, a circle with a diameter of 1 unit.

As early as 2000 B.C., the Babylonians *knew* that π was more than 3! Their estimate for π was $3\frac{1}{8}$. By the fifth century, Chinese mathematician Tsu Chung-Chi wrote that π was somewhere between 3.1415926 and 3.1415927. From 1436 until 1874, the known value of π went from 14 places past the decimal to 707 places. Computers have been used to calculate millions more digits, and today we know that the digits will never repeat and will never end. This kind of number is called *irrational*.

7.5 Replacing Trees

In large cities filled with streets and concrete buildings, trees are a valuable part of the environment. In New York City, people who damage or destroy a tree are required by law to plant new trees as community service. Two replacement rules have been used:

Diameter rule: The total *diameter* of the new tree(s) must equal the diameter of the tree(s) that were damaged or destroyed.

Area rule: The total *area of the cross section* of the new tree(s) must equal the area of the cross section of the tree(s) that were damaged or destroyed.

Problem 7.5

The following diagram shows the cross section of a damaged tree and the cross section of the new trees that will be planted to replace it.

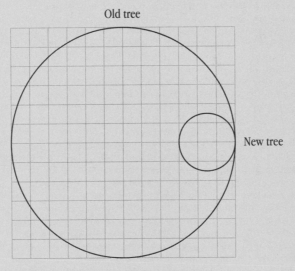

Old tree

New tree

A. How many new trees must be planted if the diameter rule is applied?

B. How many new trees must be planted if the area rule is applied?

■ Problem 7.5 Follow-Up

Which rule do you think is fairer? Use mathematics to explain your answer.

As you work on these ACE questions, use your calculator whenever you need it.

Applications

In 1–5, use the given measurements of a circle to find the other measurements. You may want to make scale drawings on grid paper to help find the missing measurements.

1. A dinner plate has a diameter of about 9 inches. Find its circumference and area.

2. A bicycle wheel is about 26 inches in diameter. Find its radius, circumference, and area.

3. A soft-drink can is about 2.25 inches in diameter. What is its circumference?

4. If the spray from a lawn sprinkler makes a circle 40 feet in radius, what are the approximate diameter, circumference, and area of the circle of lawn watered?

5. A standard long-playing record album has a 12-inch diameter; a compact disc has a 5-inch diameter. Find the radius, circumference, and area of each.

In 6–8, estimate, as accurately as possible, the area and perimeter of the figure. Make your measurements in centimeters.

6.

7.

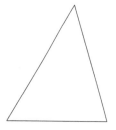

8.

Connections

Some everyday circular objects are commonly described by giving their radius or diameter. In 9–12, explain what useful information (if any) you would get from calculating the area or circumference of the circle.

9. a 3.5-inch-diameter computer disk

10. a 21-inch-diameter bicycle wheel

11. a 12-inch-diameter water pipe

12. a lawn sprinkler that sprays a 15-meter-radius section of lawn

Did you know?

3.1415926535897932384626433832795028841971693993751 0 . . . How many places can you remember? One man was known to have memorized π to 50,000 places! How important is it to be exact about this number? Actually, precision engines can be built using an approximation of 3.1416. You can calculate the earth's circumference within a fraction of an inch by knowing π out to only 10 places. So unless you love to memorize, 3.14 or the fraction $\frac{22}{7}$ are close enough approximations to make pretty good measurements.

13. A large burner on a standard electric stove is about 8 inches in diameter.

    a. What are the radius, area, and circumference of the burner?

    b. How would the area and circumference of a smaller 4-inch-diameter burner compare to the area and circumference of the 8-inch burner? Check your answers with calculations.

14. Karl and Aimeé are building a playhouse for their little sister. The floor of the playhouse will be a rectangle that is 6 feet by $8\frac{1}{2}$ feet.

    a. How much carpeting will Karl and Aimeé need to cover the floor?

    b. How much molding will they need around the edges of the floor to hold the carpet in place?

    c. The walls will be 6 feet high. A pint of paint covers about 50 square feet. How much paint will they need to paint the inside walls? Explain your answer.

    d. Make your own plan for a playhouse. Figure out how much carpeting, wood, paint, and molding you would need to build the playhouse.

15. Which measurement of a circular pizza—diameter, radius, circumference, or area—best indicates its size?

16. The Logo instructions on the following page draw a polygon with so many sides that it looks like a circle.

    a. How many sides does this polygon have?

    b. What is the perimeter of the polygon, in turtle steps?

    c. *Approximately* how many turtle steps would it take for the turtle to walk the path from point A to point B? Explain your answer.

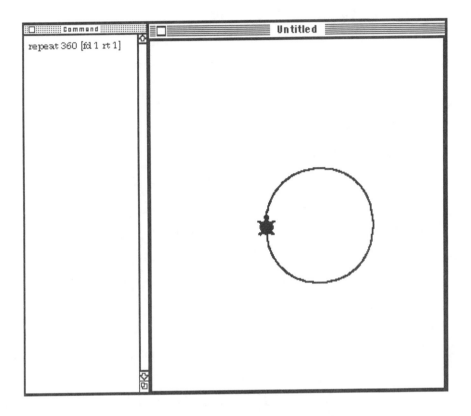

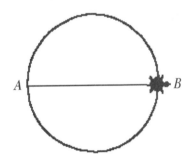

Extensions

17. Suppose you tie together the ends of a piece of string to form a loop that is 60 centimeters long.

  a. Suppose you arranged the string to form an equilateral triangle. What would the area of the enclosed space be? What would the area be if you formed square? A regular hexagon?

  Think back to the work you did in *Shapes and Designs.* Why do you think the surface of a honeycomb is covered with hexagons?

  b. Of all the rectangles with a perimeter of 60 centimeters, which has greatest area?

  c. Of all the triangles with a perimeter of 60 centimeters, which has greatest area?

  d. How does the area of a regular octagon with a perimeter of 60 centimeters compare to the areas of a triangle, a square, and a hexagon with perimeters of 60 centimeters?

  e. What happens to the enclosed area as the 60-centimeter perimeter is used to make regular polygons of more and more sides? (If you have access to a computer and the Logo programming language, you might use the computer to draw these figures.)

  f. As the number of sides of a polygon gets larger and larger, what shape does the polygon eventually resemble?

Mathematical Reflections

In this investigation, you discovered strategies for finding the area and circumference (perimeter) of a circle. You examined relationships between the circumference and the diameter of a circle and between the area and the radius of a circle. These questions will help you summarize what you have learned:

1. Describe how you can find the circumference of a circle by measuring the radius or the diameter. If you need to, explain your thinking by using a specific circle.

2. Describe how you can find the area of a circle by measuring its radius or its diameter. If you need to, explain your thinking by using a specific circle. Why is your method useful?

Think about your answers to these questions, discuss your ideas with other students and your teacher, and then write a summary of your findings in your journal.

You will soon be designing your layout for the city park. How might your new information about circles help you? What objects in your park might be in the shape of a circle—a flower garden, a water fountain?

Plan a Park

At the beginning of this unit, you read about Dr. Doolittle's donation of land to the city, which she designated as a new park. It is now time to design your plan for the piece of land. Use the information you have collected about parks, plus what you learned from your study of this unit, to prepare your final design.

Your design should satisfy the following constraints:

- The park should be rectangular with dimensions 120 yards by 100 yards.
- About half of the park should consist of a picnic area and a playground, but these two sections need not be located together.
- The picnic area should contain a circular flower garden. There should also be a garden in at least one other place in the park.
- There should be trees in several places in the park. Young trees will be planted, so your design should show room for the trees to grow.
- The park must appeal to families, so there should be more than just a picnic area and a playground.

Your design package should be neat, clear, and easy to follow. Your design should be drawn and labeled in black and white. In addition to a scale drawing of your design for the park, your project should include a report that gives:

1. the size (dimensions) of each item. These items should include gardens, trees, picnic tables, playground equipment, and anything else you included in your design.
2. the amount of land needed for each item and the calculations you used to determine the amount of land needed.

3. the materials needed. Include the amount of each item needed and the calculations you did to determine the amounts. Include the number and type of each piece of playground equipment, the amount of fencing, the numbers of picnic tables and trash containers, the amount of land covered by concrete or blacktop (so the developers can determine how much cement or blacktop will be needed), and the quantities of other items you included in your park.

4. a letter to Dr. Doolittle explaining why she should choose your design for the park. Include a justification for the choices you made about the size and quantity of items in your park.

Unit Reflections

Working on problems in this unit helped you to understand *area* and *perimeter*. You learned efficient strategies for estimating and calculating the area and perimeter of figures such as triangles, rectangles, parallelograms, and circles. You used these strategies to investigate the relationship between area and perimeter of simple polygons.

Using Your Understanding of Area and Perimeter—Test your understanding and skill in working with area and perimeter by solving the following problems.

1 *The diagram below shows a hexagon drawn on a grid.*

   a. Find the area of the hexagon.

   b. Describe two different strategies for calculating the area—one that makes use of area strategies for familiar polygons and another that does not.

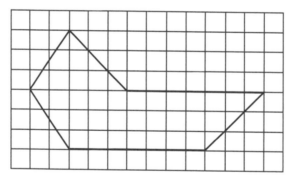

2 *In parts a–d, you are given directions for making different shapes. In each case, answer these questions.*

   i. Is it possible to make a shape with the specified properties? If so, sketch the shape.

   ii. If it is possible to make one shape with the specified properties, is it possible to draw different shapes with the same properties? If so, sketch some other possibilities.

a. a triangle with an area of 16 cm^2 and a height of 2 cm

b. a rectangle with a perimeter of 20 cm

c. a parallelogram with a pair of opposite sides of length 10 cm and an area of 96 cm^2

d. a rectangle with perimeter of 24 cm and area of 20 cm^2

3 *The Smith's living room floor is a square 20 feet by 20 feet that is covered with parquet wood. They have carpeted a quarter-circle region as shown in this diagram.*

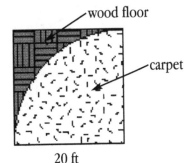

20 ft

20 ft

wood floor

carpet

a. What is the area of the **uncovered wood**, to the nearest square foot?

b. A 1-quart can of floor wax covers 30 square feet of wood flooring. How many cans of floor wax are needed to wax the uncovered wood?

c. A special finishing trim was placed along the curved edge of the carpet. How much trim, to the nearest tenth of a foot, was needed?

Explaining Your Reasoning—To answer questions about area and perimeter you have to apply properties of geometric figures and then use strategies to make numerical estimates or calculations.

1. How would you explain the difference between area and perimeter to a younger student who has not yet studied those mathematical ideas?

2. Describe calculation strategies that can be used to find the area of each shape and be prepared to justify each procedure.

a. Rectangle

width

length

b. Triangle

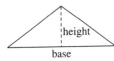

height

base

c. Parallelogram

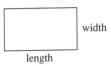

height

base

d. Circle

radius

diameter

3. How would you estimate the area and perimeter of an irregular figure such as the one drawn on the grid below? What is a reasonable estimate for the area of this particular figure?

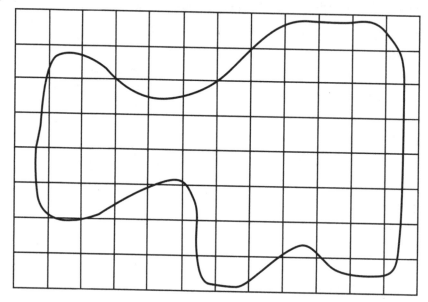

Area and perimeter are among the most useful concepts for measuring the size of geometric figures. You will use strategies for estimating and calculating the size of geometric figures in many future units of *Connected Mathematics*, especially those that deal with surface area and volume of solid figures, similarity, and the Pythagorean Theorem. You will also find that area and volume estimates and calculations are required in a variety of practical and technical problems.

Glossary

area The measure of the amount of surface enclosed by the sides of a figure. To find the area of a figure, you can count how many unit squares it takes to cover the figure. You can find the area of a rectangle by multiplying the length by the width. This is simply a shortcut method for finding the number of unit squares it takes to cover the rectangle. If a figure has curved or irregular sides, you can estimate the area by covering the surface with a grid and counting whole grid squares and parts of grid squares. When you find the area of a shape, write the units, such as square feet or cm², to indicate the unit square that was used to find the area. The area of the square below is 9 square units, and the area of the rectangle is 6 square units.

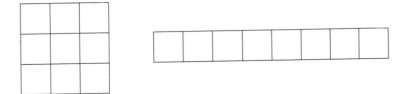

circle A two-dimensional object in which every point is the same distance from a point (not on the circle) called the *center*. Point *C* is the center of the circle below.

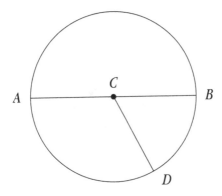

circumference The distance around (or perimeter of) a circle. It takes slightly more than three diameters to match the circumference of a circle. More formally, the circumference of a circle is pi (π) times the diameter of the circle. Pi is the mathematical name for the ratio of a circle's circumference to its diameter. This ratio is the same for every circle, and is approximately equal to 3.1416.

diameter A segment that goes from one point on a circle, through the center, to another point on the circle. The length of this segment is also called the diameter. In the definition of circle on page 87, segment *AB* is a diameter.

linear dimensions Linear measurements, such as length, width, base, and height, which describe the size of figures. The longest dimension or the dimension along the bottom of a rectangle is usually called the *length*, and the other dimension is called the *width*, but it is not incorrect to reverse these labels. The word *base* is used when talking about triangles and parallelograms. The *base* is usually measured along a horizontal side, but it is sometimes convenient to think of one of the other sides as the base. For a triangle, the height is the perpendicular distance from the vertex opposite the base to the base. For a parallelogram, the height is the perpendicular distance from a point on the side opposite the base to the base You need to be flexible when you encounter these terms, so you are able to determine their meanings from the context of the situation.

perimeter The measure of the distance around a figure. Perimeter is a measure of length. To find the perimeter of a figure, you count the number of unit lengths it takes to surround the figure. When you find the perimeter of a shape, write the units (such as centimeters, feet, or yards) to indicate the unit that was used to find the perimeter. The perimeter of the square on page 87 is 12 units, because 12 units of length surround the figure. The perimeter of the rectangle is 18 units. Notice that the rectangle has a larger perimeter, but a smaller area, than the square.

perpendicular lines Lines that meet at right angles. The length and width of a rectangle are perpendicular to each other and the base and height of a triangle are perpendicular to each other. In diagrams, perpendicular lines are often indicated by drawing a small square where the lines meet.

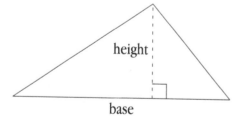

radius A segment from the center of a circle to a point on the circle. The length of this segment is also called the radius. The radius is half of the diameter. In the definition of circle on page 87, *CD* is one radius. The plural of radius is radii. All the radii of a circle have the same length

Glosario

área La medida de la cantidad de superficie encerrada por los lados de una figura. Para hallar el área de una figura, puedes contar cuántas unidades cuadradas se requieren para cubrir la figura. Puedes hallar el área de un rectángulo multiplicando el largo por el ancho. Esto es sencillamente un método más corto para hallar el número de unidades cuadradas requeridas para cubrir el rectángulo. Si una figura tiene lados curvos o irregulares, puedes estimar el área cubriendo la superficie con una cuadrícula y contando los cuadrados enteros y las partes de cuadrados en la cuadrícula. Cuando halles el área de una figura, escribe las unidades, como ser pies cuadrados o cm^2, para indicar el tamaño de la unidad cuadrada que fue usada para hallar el área. El área del cuadrado representado a continuación es de 9 unidades cuadradas y el área del rectángulo es de 8 unidades cuadradas.

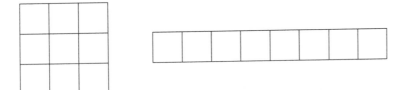

círculo Un objeto bidimensional en el que cada punto está a la misma distancia de un punto (que no está en el círculo) llamado el *centro*. El punto *C* es el centro del siguiente círculo.

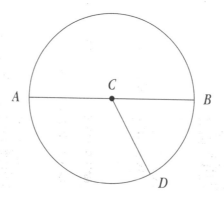

circunferencia La distancia alrededor de (o el perímetro de) un círculo. Se requiere apenas más de tres diámetros para representar la circunferencia de un círculo. Más formalmente, la circunferencia de un círculo es pi (π) multiplicado por el diámetro del círculo. Pi es el nombre matemático para la razón entre la circunferencia de un círculo y su diámetro. Esta razón es la misma para cada círculo y es aproximadamente igual a 3.1416.

diámetro Un segmento que va desde un punto en un círculo, pasando por el centro, hasta otro punto en el círculo. La longitud de este segmento también se llama "diámetro". En la definición de círculo de la página 87, el segmento *AB* es un diámetro.

dimensiones lineales Medidas lineales, como el largo, el ancho, la base y la altura, que describen el tamaño de las figuras. La dimensión más larga o la dimensión a lo largo de la parte inferior de un rectángulo generalmente se llama *largo* y la otra dimensión se llama *ancho*, pero no es incorrecto invertir estos rótulos. La palabra *base* se usa cuando se habla de triángulos y de paralelogramos. La base se mide a lo largo de un lado horizontal pero a veces es conveniente pensar en uno de los otros lados como la base. En un triángulo, la altura es la distancia perpendicular desde el vértice opuesto a la base hasta la base. En un paralelogramo, la altura es la distancia perpendicular desde un punto en el lado opuesto a la base hasta la base. Tienes que ser flexible cuando te encuentras con estos términos para que puedas determinar su significado dentro del contexto de la situación.

líneas perpendiculares Líneas que se encuentran en ángulos rectos. El largo y el ancho de un rectángulo son perpendiculares entre sí, y la base y la altura de un triángulo son perpendiculares entre sí. En los diagramas, las líneas perpendiculares generalmente se indican dibujando un pequeño cuadrado donde se unen las líneas.

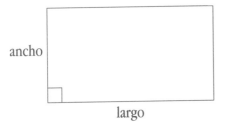

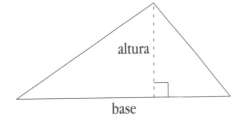

perímetro La medida de la distancia alrededor de una figura. El perímetro es una medida de longitud. Para hallar el perímetro de una figura, cuentas el número de unidades de longitud que se requieren para rodear la figura. Cuando halles el perímetro de una figura, escribe las unidades (como, por ejemplo, centímetros, pies o yardas) para indicar la unidad que se usó para hallar el perímetro. El perímetro del cuadrado que aparece en la página 87 es de 12 unidades, porque 12 unidades de longitud rodean la figura. El perímetro del rectángulo es de 18 unidades. Observa que el rectángulo tiene un perímetro más largo, pero un área más pequeña, que el cuadrado.

radio Un segmento desde el centro de un círculo hasta un punto en el círculo. La longitud de este segmento también se llama "radio". El radio es la mitad del diámetro. En la definición de círculo de la página 87, *CD* es un radio. Todos los radios de un círculo tienen la misma longitud.

Index